GREAT SMOKY MOUNTAINS

NATURAL WONDERS

Jason Cooper

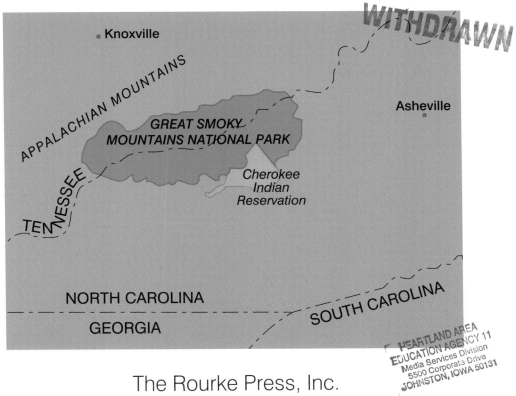

Knoxville

APPALACHIAN MOUNTAINS

Asheville

GREAT SMOKY
MOUNTAINS NATIONAL PARK

TENNESSEE

Cherokee
Indian
Reservation

NORTH CAROLINA

SOUTH CAROLINA

GEORGIA

The Rourke Press, Inc.
Vero Beach, Florida 32964

PHOTO CREDITS
Cover © Jerry Hennen; p. 4, 10, 15 © Steve Warble; p. 7, 12, 17,
21 © Lynn M. Stone; p. 13, 18 © James P. Rowan;
p. 8 © Breck P. Kent

Library of Congress Cataloging-in-Publication Data
Cooper, Jason, 1942-
   Great Smoky Mountains / Jason Cooper
      p. cm. — (Natural Wonders)
   Includes index.
   ISBN 1-57103-014-X
    1. Great Smoky Mountains (N.C. and Tenn.)—Juvenile literature.
2. Great Smoky Mountains National Park (N.C. and Tenn.)—
Juvenile literature.
[1. Great Smoky Mountains (N.C. and Tenn.) 2. Great Smoky
Mountains National Park (N.C. and Tenn.) 3. National parks and
reserves.]
I. Title II. Series: Cooper, Jason, 1942-   Natural Wonders
F443.G7.C57 1995
976.8' 89—dc20
                                   95–12304
                                    CIP
                                    AC

Printed in the USA

TABLE OF CONTENTS

The Great Smoky Mountains   5

Plants   6

Animals   9

Life in the Great Smokies   11

Great Smoky Mountain National Park   14

The Wonders of the Smokies   16

Visiting the Great Smokies   19

Seasons in the Smokies   20

People in the Smokies   22

Glossary   23

Index   24

THE GREAT SMOKY MOUNTAINS

The Great Smoky Mountains often seem to rise through a ghostly mist. That smoky look gave this range of mountains along the Tennessee-North Carolina border its name.

The Smokies are part of the Blue Ridge Mountain group in the Southern Appalachian mountain chain. The Smokies are among the tallest and most rugged mountains in the East.

Unlike many Western mountains, the Smokies' peaks are rounded and covered by dense forest.

The ghostly hills of the Smokies wear a cloak of summer green

PLANTS

The forests of the Great Smokies are the richest in the East. Over 200 **species** (SPEE sheez), or kinds, of trees live there. Much of the Great Smoky forest has never been cut.

Beneath the trees are great clumps of **rhododendron** (ro do DEN drun) shrubs. Late each spring and early summer, the white, pink, and orange rhododendron blossoms color the mountain slopes.

Threaded with brooks, the moist forest of the Great Smokies is the richest in the East

ANIMALS

The Great Smokies are a safe home for Eastern forest animals. Over 200 species of birds live in the mountains. The largest are wild turkeys. The raven, usually a bird of the Far West and North, lives in the highest country of the Great Smokies.

Whitetail deer, raccoons, opossums, red squirrels, and bobcats are among the Great Smoky animals. The largest mammal of these mountains is the black bear.

More than 20 kinds of salamanders live in and near the mountain brooks.

A young black bear rests in a mountain clearing

LIFE IN THE GREAT SMOKIES

The plants and animals of the Great Smokies live in several different communities. Many plants and animals of the lowlands do not live on the high slopes.

Hikers notice the change in wild plants and animals as they climb. The forests of **broad-leafed** (BRAWD leeft) trees are replaced by needle-leafed evergreen trees like red spruce. Gray squirrels of the broad-leafed forests are replaced by red squirrels in the evergreens.

Evergreens, like red spruce, replace broad-leafed trees on the cooler upper slopes of the Smokies

11

Behind a veil of leaves, a waterfall splashes into a mountain brook

Mountain brooks and moist woodlands are an ideal home for this red-backed salamander and several of its relatives

GREAT SMOKY MOUNTAIN NATIONAL PARK

Great Smoky Mountain National Park was created by the U.S. Government in 1930. Becoming a park protected the mountains from mining, lumbering, and other harmful uses.

Several million people visit Great Smoky Mountain National Park each year. Thousands hike the park's mountain trails, past rushing, gushing streams and forest waterfalls.

Seventy-one miles of the famous Appalachian Trail wind through the park. The entire trail travels from Georgia to Maine.

Fresh snow greets hikers on the Appalachian Trail in Great Smoky Mountains National Park

THE WONDERS OF THE SMOKIES

The Great Smokies have one of the highest points of land in the Southeast—Clingman's Dome. It rises 6,642 feet above sea level.

The national park protects the last, best piece of uncut Eastern forest remaining in the United States. In addition to the forest itself, the Great Smokies has curious mountain meadows called **balds** (BAWLDZ). Despite thick forest all around them, balds are grassy and shrubby.

Catawba rhododendron blooms on a grassy mountain bald

VISITING THE GREAT SMOKIES

Paved roads through the Great Smokies lead to many interesting and scenic places. An 11-mile loop road at Cade's Cove travels past old farms and pioneer **homesteads** (HOME stedz). Another road travels within one-half mile of an observation tower at Clingman's Dome.

Great Smoky Mountains National Park has 600 miles of foot and horse trails. Trails climb from moist, broad-leafed woodland into high evergreen forest.

Dogwood blooms behind the cabin of pioneer John Oliver in Cade's Cove

SEASONS IN THE SMOKIES

Each spring the Great Smokies bloom with a remarkable display of wildflowers. Flowers blossom first in the lower places. As spring advances, flowers bloom in higher places. One of the Smokies' most beautiful wildflowers is the lady's-slipper orchid.

Songbirds traveling north move through the Smokies in spring and return on their autumn, southbound flight.

Fall is exciting in the Smokies. Broad-leafed trees turn red and yellow before shedding their leaves. Each winter, snow covers the high ground.

Pink lady's-slippers bloom each spring in Great Smoky Mountains National Park

PEOPLE IN THE SMOKIES

Native American Cherokees were among the first settlers in the Great Smokies. In the 1800's, fighting between Cherokees and white settlers led to the removal of the Cherokees.

American soldiers in 1839 forced as many as 17,000 Cherokees to move from the southern Appalachians to Oklahoma. Thousands of Cherokees died on the long journey in what became known as the Trail of Tears.

A few Cherokees remained in the Smokies. Cherokee land borders Great Smoky Mountain National Park today.

Glossary

balds (BAWLDZ) — grassy, treeless openings surrounded by mountain forest in the Southern Appalachians

broad-leafed (BRAWD leeft) — referring to trees with wide leaves, such as maples, sycamores, and elms; leaves that are shed in the fall

homestead (HOME sted) — a family's home and land

rhododendron (ro do DEN drun) — any of several related shrubs with bright flowers and leathery, evergreen leaves

species (SPEE sheez) — a certain kind of plant or animal within a closely related group; for example, a *maple* tree

INDEX

animals   9, 11
Appalachian Trail   14
balds   16
bear, black   9
birds   9
Blue Ridge Mountains   5
Cade's Cove   19
Cherokees   22
Clingmans's Dome   16, 19
fall   20
forests   5, 6, 11, 16, 19
Great Smoky Mountains
   National Park   14, 19
mist   5
plants   6, 11

rhododendron   6
salamanders   9
Southern Appalachian
   Mountains   5, 22
spring   20
squirrel
   gray   11
   red   11
Trail of Tears   22
trails   14, 19
trees   6, 11
U.S. Government   14
wildflowers   20
winter   20